MURDERE  S
THE LIGHT...

Ex-murderer Saul from Tarsus sees the light on the road to Damascus. Picture: James P Smith

A man was struck blind after a flash of light fell from the sky.

The man, known as Saul of Tarsus was on his way to Damascus when the incident happened. He had intended to arrest followers of Jesus, before he was stopped.

It is reported that Saul heard a voice from heaven speaking to him. Witnesses who were with him at the time, also saw the bright light.

When asked who had spoken to him, Saul said that it was Jesus, the man he hated. He asked why Saul was so against him and told him to get up and go into the city.

(Story continued on page 4)

SAUL BEFORE...

Saul being handed letters to arrest Christians in Damascus.

PAUL AFTER

Paul seen preaching to Jews in a synagogue in Damascus

Pictures: James P Smith

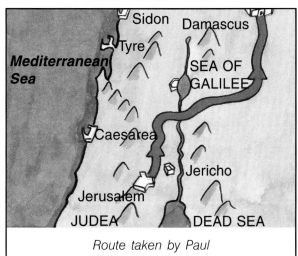

Route taken by Paul

(Continued from page 3)

The other travellers who were with Saul had to lead him into the city, where he remained for three days.

A man called Ananias was seemingly told by God to visit Saul. On his arrival, Ananias placed his hands on Saul's head and prayed with him. Saul (now known as Paul), was now able to see and was filled with the Holy Spirit.

It seems that this experience has changed Saul dramatically. Since the event he has been seen preaching in synagogues that Jesus is the son of God. Many people are suspicious of his behaviour and can hardly believe he is the same man.

Jews in the area have been so upset by his preaching, that plans have been made to kill him. The man who formerly murdered Christians for their faith is now being threatened by his own people.

Christian friends have been guarding him night and day to protect him from danger.

PARDON ME?

The growing number of followers of Jesus has led to the creation of several new words. To help readers understand more about the movement we have explained them for you:

Christian:
A person who loves Jesus and follows his teaching. The name was first used at a place called Antioch.

Holy Spirit:
Given to Christians to help them become more like Jesus.

Jesus the Healer

It was discovered that the woman who had touched Jesus had been suffering from an incurable illness for twelve years. She was healed after touching Jesus.

Picture: Neil Pinchbeck

(story continued from page 1)

Family home in Capernaum. Picture: Fred Apps

the man Jesus, who is thought to have healing power. After begging Jesus to help him, the two men made their way to Jairus' home.

Their journey was delayed by a large crowd.

Suddenly Jesus stopped and asked who had touched him. A woman came forward. While they were speaking, a messenger arrived with tragic news - Jairus' child was dead.

On arriving at the house, people were crying and wailing. Jesus told everyone to wait outside, apart from the parents and Jesus' followers. Jesus said that the child was only sleeping. People just laughed at him.

However not long after, the girl was seen alive eating some food. It is reported that Jesus had just taken her hand and told her to get up. There is much excitement in the town at this amazing miracle.

Tax man gives money away

Local people still in shock

PEOPLE in Jericho were recently surprised by the strange actions of a wealthy tax collector.

The man, whose name is Zacchaeus is well-known for being a cheat. He was recently witnessed paying back up to four times the amount of money he had stolen. These actions were watched in disbelief by neighbours.

Zacchaeus seen handing out money to local tax payers. Picture: Neil Pinchbeck

Being a small man, Zacchaeus climbed a nearby sycamore tree in order to see over the crowd.

This event happened soon after the visit of Jesus of Nazareth, the man who claims to be the Son of God. The streets of Jericho were lined with crowds of people, who were waiting to see Jesus. Being a small man, Zacchaeus climbed a nearby sycamore tree in order to see over the crowd.

Suddenly Jesus stood beside the tree, looked up at Zacchaeus and asked him to come down, as he wished to visit the tax collector's home. Zacchaeus came down immediately, and

Streets of Jericho lined with people waiting for Jesus. Sycamore tree climbed by Zacchaeus in background. Picture: Neil Pinchbeck

appeared to be happy at this request.

However, various people in the crowd were heard muttering disapproval at the company Jesus had chosen.

Soon after meeting with Jesus, Zacchaeus was seen giving away large sums of money. It seems that the man Jesus has an amazing effect on the lives of many people. Whose life will he be changing next?

Zacchaeus Profile

JOB:	Tax collector
SIZE:	Small in height
HOME:	Jericho
FRIENDS:	Few
BEFORE he met Jesus...	Known as a cheat
AFTER he met Jesus...	Changed man, giving away large sums of money.

CROWD OF 5,000 FED WITH 5 LOAVES & 2 FISH!

Today by the banks of the Sea of Galilee, over 5,000 people were fed with only 5 loaves of bread and 2 small fish.

The crowd had gathered to listen to the famous speaker, Jesus of Nazareth. Men, women and children travelled from villages near and far to hear his teaching.

As the day wore on, Jesus told his disciples to feed the people. There were no shops or houses nearby for his disciples to buy food for the hungry crowd.

One young boy came forward and gave his lunch to Jesus' followers. Jesus took the food, and told

The young boy who gave his small picnic to Jesus. Picture: Colin King

everyone to sit down on the grass. He gave thanks for the bread and fish and then told his disciples to give the food to the people. Incredibly the small picnic fed over 5,000 people, with twelve baskets full of leftovers! What a miracle - what will this man Jesus do next?

SLEEPY MAN FALLS OUT OF WINDOW

Paul speaking to the people about Christianity.

Eutychus after fall from third storey window.

Keen friends wave goodbye as Paul leaves for his trip abroad.

Pictures: James P Smith

A farewell dinner in Troas almost ended in tragedy after one of the guests fell from the upstairs window.

The special guest speaker, Paul from Tarsus had been invited to speak to the group of Christians, before leaving for a trip abroad.

Relaxing after the evening meal, the people were encouraged by the teaching of Paul. After listening to Paul for several hours, one of the young men called Eutychus, grew so tired he fell asleep. Unfortunately he was sitting on the third storey window ledge at the time and fell over the edge.

The people rushed out of the house to pick him up but discovered that the fall had killed him. Paul went over to the man, threw himself on top of him and declared that he was alive. Paul then returned upstairs and continued talking until daylight. The tired man was taken home to be looked after by friends.

RIOT BREAKS OUT IN EPHESUS

Angry mob seen fighting on the streets of Ephesus. Pictures: James P Smith

Example of god made by local silversmiths. Picture: Fred Apps

The city of Ephesus has been disturbed by street fighting. The violence began when an argument broke out between the preacher Paul and some local workers. It seems that Paul had made certain statements which could put the men out of business.

Ephesus is full of man-made statues and gods, which are worshipped by the people. Paul said that this practice was wrong and that the gods were false. A group of silversmiths, who

The preacher Paul arguing with local silversmiths, who produce man-made gods

make the gods were not happy with Paul and knew that his teaching could ruin their business. One man called Demetrius told the people that Paul was wrong to say bad things about the goddess Artemis.

Immediately the crowd started to get angry and the city was in uproar. Paul was in danger of being attacked and was told to stay away from the crowd. However, two of his friends were taken by the mob to a local meeting place. Many of the people did not even know what had caused the riot, but joined in anyway.

The riot would have continued if the town-clerk had not stepped in. He managed to use peace talks to calm the crowd and told them that if they had a problem they should go to court, not argue in the street. His blunt talking worked and the crowd soon disappeared. The riot was over.

DOCTORS BAFFLED BY HEALINGS

Doctors are confused by reports of people who have been healed from illness. The reports have come from various sources but have one thing in common - they all involve the man Jesus. The following stories record the life-changing effect of Jesus' healing touch.

CASE 1 - IN DECAPOLIS

A man who was deaf and had difficulty in speaking was brought to Jesus.

He took the man away from the crowd, put his fingers in his ears and touched his tongue. Jesus then sighed and said, 'Be opened.' At that very moment the man began to speak and was able to hear.

Pictures: Neil Stewart

CASE 2 - IN BETHSAIDA

A blind man was brought to Jesus. Once again Jesus took the man out of the village to a quiet place. After spitting on the man's eyes Jesus asked the man if he could see. The man was able to see some objects but not clearly. Jesus placed his hands one more time on the man's eyes. This time the man who had been blind could now see.

CASE 3 - IN CAPERNAUM

Jesus was approached by messengers from a Roman officer whose servant was very sick. He was unable to walk and was lying at home, in the officer's house.

Without being asked, Jesus told the messengers he would go and make the servant better.

However to Jesus' surprise, the officer sent friends to tell him that he didn't deserve to have Jesus come to his house. The officer believed that if Jesus just said the word his servant would be well. Although Jesus was taken aback by the officer's word, he told him that what he believed would take place.

When the messengers returned, they discovered the servant had been cured at the very same hour Jesus had spoken.

MAN GOES THROUGH THE ROOF

A house in Capernaum was seriously overcrowded, when crowds of people pushed inside to hear Jesus of Nazareth.

Whilst Jesus was teaching the people who had gathered together, a hole began to appear in the roof. The hole grew bigger and bigger, until a man on a mat was lowered through the roof.

Crowds push into house to see Jesus.

Friends lower man through hole in the roof.

Pictures: Neil Pinchbeck

Jesus welcomed the man and his four friends. He was touched by their desire to see him and their belief that he could heal their crippled friend. Looking at the crippled man Jesus said, 'Your sins are forgiven.'

Some of the people in the crowd, the teachers of the Law and the Pharisees, were angry with Jesus and thought that he had no right to speak these words. Jesus seemed to know what they were thinking. He then told the man to take up his

The man walking after the miracle.

BUSINESS WOMAN BAPTISED

A business woman's life was transformed after she listened to Christian teaching.

mat and walk. In full view of everyone, the man did just that. The crowd were amazed at this miracle and praised God for what had happened.

Lydia, who deals in the purple cloth trade, lives in Philippi. Although she has been a worshipper of God for some time, she took the decison to be baptised, after speaking to the missionary preacher Paul.

Many women had gathered together for prayer by the riverside when Paul arrived.

Other members of Lydia's family were also affected and were baptised with her.

WHAT IS BAPTISM?
* an outward sign using water which tells others the person has turned away from sin and has become a Christian.
* a practice encouraged by the prophet called 'John the Baptist.'

Lydia gathers with other women to pray by the river. Paul takes the opportunity to preach. Picture: James P Smith

EARTHQUAKE SHOCKS PRISON

Prison doors fly open at Philippi prison after violent earthquake. Pictures James P Smith

THE PRISON IN PHILIPPI

was recently shaken up by a violent earthquake. The prison warden was about to kill himself when he discovered that all the doors were open. However, not one of the prisoners had escaped.

It has been reported that two prisoners, the preacher Paul and his friend Silas, had been singing at the time of the earthquake. They had been beaten and flung into prison after commanding an evil spirit to leave a young slave girl. Her owners had been furious by this action, which had put them out of business. The girl was now no longer able to predict the future.

After being placed in a cell and bound with chains and wooden stocks the two men seemed to rejoice in their situation - an unusual reaction.

The prison warden, who had fallen asleep, was woken by the earthquake and panicked when he saw the doors lying wide open. Just as he raised his sword to kill himself, Paul and Silas shouted at him to stop. The warden was amazed when he heard all the prisoners were still inside.

The prison warden began to tremble and asked Paul what he should do to be saved. Paul explained the Christian message, known as 'the Gospel,' to him. The man immediately told the good news to his family and they were all baptised. The warden's attitude to Paul and Silas had completely changed and he now invited them to his home, where he fed them and looked after their wounds.

Paul shares the Christian message with the prison warden's family.

Money found in fish's mouth

A STRANGE STORY was told by collectors of the temple tax in Capernaum. When a man called Simon Peter went to pay his taxes, it was discovered that he had found the money in the mouth of a fish.

The man had gone fishing after being told by his teacher, Jesus, to go to the lake and open the mouth of the first fish he caught. Simon, a former fisherman left his trade to follow Jesus.

MAN HAS POWER OVER WEATHER

Local fishermen in the Sea of Galilee were shocked when a man calmed a storm by just speaking to it.

The men had been out in the lake at night when the storm took place. Jesus of Nazareth had been asleep in the boat when his friends woke him up in fear. They were upset that he did not seem to be aware of the storm.

Jesus then told the wind and the waves to be calm and still. The weather changed as soon as he spoke. The fishermen were scared by the power of this man.

WATER TURNS INTO WINE

Wedding guests are amazed!

Servant girl fills jars with water.
Pictures: Jennifer Stevenson

A miracle took place in Cana in Galilee when jars of water were turned into wine. The wedding hosts began to panic when they realised they had run out of wine.

One of the guests, Jesus of Nazareth, was present with his mother Mary. Being aware of problem, she had asked her son if he could help. At first he did not seem too keen but later rose and went to speak to the servants. Jesus then told the servants to take six stone water jars and to fill them full of water. The servants obeyed and took the jars to the host of the wedding party.

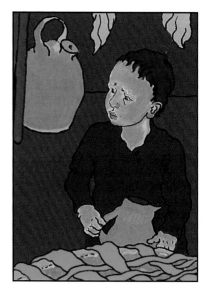

He was surprised by how good the wine tasted and praised the bridegroom. However, he did wonder why the bridegroom had left all the good wine till the end of the party. The man Jesus is keeping quiet about this remarkable miracle, but news is spreading fast.

SHIPWRECK!

Storm blows ship to pieces

Sailors try desperately to keep the ship under control.
Pictures: James P Smith

Prisoners swim ashore to Malta

A ship carrying prisoners to Rome was wrecked by a wild storm at sea. No-one was killed but the 276 survivors were badly shaken by the experience.

A strong wind, known as the 'North-Easter' blew the ship past the Island of Crete. After losing total control of the ship, the crew let the wind carry them towards land. It is reported that one of the prisoners on board, Paul, had warned the crew that the weather was not suitable for sailing, but they did not take his advice.

Cargo was thrown overboard in an attempt to survive. All the sailors were gripped with fear, apart from Paul whose faith in God gave hope in the terrifying situation. He told the men that an angel from God had spoken to him and said that everyone would be kept alive.

(continued on page 20)

(Story continued from page 19)

'...not even a hair of your head will be lost...'

After travelling for fourteen days the men dropped the ship's anchors and prepared to run the ship aground. Unfortunately the ship struck a sand-bar and was destroyed.

The soldiers had planned to kill the prisoners who were on board to stop them escaping. However the men jumped into the sea and swam ashore to safety.

The Islanders of Malta were surprised to see hundreds of men coming out of the water but gave them a warm welcome. Arrangements have yet to be made to transport the survivors to Rome.

DESERT MAN TURNS PREACHER

Crowds of people are going out to the desert to listen to a preacher.

The man, called John the Baptist, is reported to live in the desert. He survives on a healthy diet of locusts and wild honey and wears simple styled clothes made from camel's hair.

His message to those that come, is that they need do the following:

* To turn away from all wrongdoing. (sin)
* Be baptised in the River Jordan.
* Change the way they live, share what they have and be fair to others.

He has also mentioned the arrival of someone else, who is greater than he is.

This person will baptise people, but not with water. He will baptise with the Holy Spirit. The crowds are wondering who this new prophet will be. There is talk that this new prophet could actually be the Messiah.

DEAD OR ALIVE?
Mystery remains unsolved

The two men who claim to have seen Jesus ran all the way back to Jerusalem to tell his followers the news. Picture: Neil Stewart

Startling reports that Jesus of Nazareth is alive have shocked the nation.

The teacher, who claims to be the son of God, was killed by crucifixion in front of hundreds of witnesses last week.

Many people thought his death would be the end of the road for his followers. However, recent reports have shown that belief in Jesus' claims have grown.

Two followers told reporters that a man had started walking with them on the road to Emmaus. They had been so deep in discussion that they didn't recognise him.

belief in Jesus' claims have grown...

The person had asked them what they had been talking about. They were amazed to discover that he had not heard about the death of Jesus.

On arriving at Emmaus they encouraged the man to be their guest. Just as they were about to eat, the man took the bread, gave thanks and gave it to them.

(continued on page 22)

MEN GIVE UP JOBS OF A LIFE-TIME

There could soon be a shortage of fishermen if a current trend continues. Men are being called away from the only jobs they have ever known to follow a man called Jesus.

Four men from the region of Galilee have just left their boats and families to take up new work.

Two brothers, Peter and Andrew were the first to follow Jesus. They had been preparing to go fishing when Jesus called to them. He told them to leave their nets and to start fishing for something else - people!

Further on down the beach two other brothers James and John were out in their boat, already at work. Again Jesus called out to them and invited them to work for him. They didn't even hesitate but left their father in the boat to go with Jesus.

DEAD OR ALIVE
(continued from page 21)

At that moment their eyes were opened and they realised the man was actually Jesus! Just then, Jesus disappeared from sight. They were so excited about the discovery that they immediately set off back to Jerusalem to tell others.

Further reports are still being received which leaves the mystery unsolved. Is Jesus dead or alive?

Picture: Fred Apps

PIGS JUMP OVER CLIFF EDGE

Frightened pig herders watch pigs disappear over the edge of the cliff. Picture: Neil Pinchbeck

A herd of pigs drowned in the Sea of Galilee after leaping over the edge of a cliff.

After investigating the reason for this strange behaviour it was discovered that a local madman was involved in the case.

The man who is from the area of Gergesa in Galilee had for many years lived among tombs, running around like a wild animal. He was thought to behave like this because evil spirits (demons) lived inside him.

The arrival of Jesus of Nazareth sent the man into a frenzy. Jesus then commanded the evil spirits to come out of the man. The spirits then jumped into the pigs who ran down the hillside.

The men who had been looking after the pigs got such a fright that they ran away to the local town and told the people there what had happened.

A crowd went out to find the madman whom they saw now calmly sitting at the feet of Jesus. The people were so afraid of Jesus' power that they asked him to leave the area.

The man who was no longer mad returned to his home telling the people how Jesus had set him free from the evil spirits.

ANGEL HELPS PRISONER ESCAPE

A prisoner's dream came true when an angel helped him to escape.

The prisoner, called Peter was put in prison for being a Christian.

During the middle of the night, while the man lay sleeping, a bright light suddenly shone in his cell. An angel appeared and touched Peter and told him to get up quickly. Instantly the chains fell from his arms and he was able to move. The angel then told him to get dressed, put on his cloak and follow him. Peter thought he was dreaming, but did as he was told.

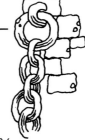

PRISON CONDITIONS

People are often put in prison for the following reasons:
* Not paying money which they owe
* Committing a crime
* For being a follower of Jesus

SECURITY
Prisoners are well guarded and held in cells using:
* Stocks holding the prisoner's ankles, wrist or both in place
* Chains

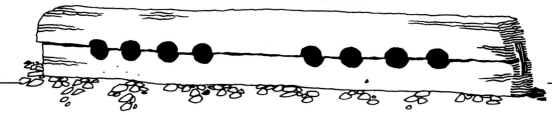

(story continued from page 24)

They walked past the guards who did not see or hear them. As they came to the iron gate which led to the city, the gate seemed to open by itself. The angel left Peter shortly after. The ex-prisoner believes the angel was sent by God to rescue him from King Herod.

WISE MEN LOOK FOR NEW KING

The special star seen by the Wise Men

Pictures: Neil Stewart

King Herod meets with his own wise men

The arrival of some important wise men from **the East has caused a stir in the Palace.**

King Herod is reported to be upset by a major discovery. A special star seen in the East shows that a new king has been born. The wise men have come to the area to worship this new king.

King Herod called a meeting with his own wise men to see if they had heard the news. He was later told that the new king was to be born in Bethlehem. This fact had apparently been predicted a long time ago by prophets.

(story continued on page 26)

PRIEST STRUCK DUMB

Priest tries to speak to crowd using sign language after losing his speech.
Picture: Neil Stewart

A priest who was on duty in the temple in Jerusalem was struck dumb.

It was his turn to go into the temple and burn incense. While he performed this important job, other worshippers were outside the temple praying.

After a long time there was still no sign of the priest Zechariah. Some people began to worry about his safety.

When he did eventually appear, he could no longer speak. It is reported that he had seen a vision while in the temple. Using sign language, the priest tried to describe what had happened. No one knows whether this man will ever speak again.

Wise men - last seen leaving the palace. Picture: Neil Stewart

The King told the wise men to find this new king and to return to the palace with the news. It is believed the men were carrying expensive gifts to give to the baby king.

However, the King heard no word from the wise men as they did not return to the palace.

MAN LOSES HEAD AFTER KING'S PARTY

The preacher John the Baptist was killed last night after a party at the palace.

Herodias' daughter dancing for king.
Pictures: Neil Pinchbeck

King upset by the death of John

John had been put in the palace prison for speaking against King Herod's behaviour. The King had married his brother's wife. The King's wife, Herodias, wanted John put to death but Herod would not allow it. He liked to listen to his teaching and often spent time talking with John.

Herodias got her chance for revenge on the King's birthday. Her daughter danced so well for Herod, that he promised her anything she wanted. When she asked for the head of John the Baptist he was very upset.

However, Herod had made a promise and could not break it in front of his famous guests.

LOCAL TEMPLE TURNED INTO MARKET PLACE

The man called Jesus has made startling claims that the temple in Jerusalem belongs to his Father.

Traders seen buying and selling in the temple. Pictures: Neil Stewart

Temple

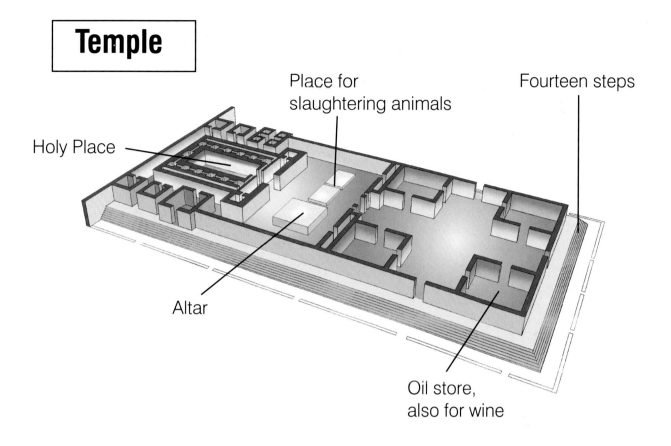

Place for slaughtering animals

Fourteen steps

Holy Place

Altar

Oil store, also for wine

Jesus was furious when he discovered people were going to the temple, not to pray, but to buy and sell goods. He said it was being turned into a den of thieves.

He began turning over the tables and chairs where money changers and sellers sat. He would not let anyone else enter the building who intended to make money out of the stalls.

Crowd amazed by Jesus' words and actions...

The Chief Priests and teachers of the law were extremely upset by Jesus' behaviour. Rumours are spreading that they are afraid of this man and intend to have him killed.

The crowds who watched the event were amazed by Jesus' words and actions. He has made a strong impression in the city.

MAN'S FEET WASHED IN PERFUME BATH

Disciples claim money should have been given to the poor

Whilst preparing for the Passover feast, the town of Bethany witnessed an unusual event.

It was reported that the man called Jesus was having a quiet meal with friends when a visitor arrived unexpectedly.

A woman called Mary entered the room and approached Jesus directly. She took an expensive alabaster jar, full of perfume, and poured it over his feet. As the strong smell filled the room, Jesus' followers (called disciples) were annoyed and claimed that the perfume had been wasted. It should have been sold and the money given to the poor.

Jesus responded by saying the woman had done something very special, which was in preparation for his burial. This man Jesus seems very certain that he is about to die.

Picture: Neil Pinchbeck

SHOCK AS BABY IS GIVEN UNUSUAL NAME

SPECIAL FACTS ABOUT THE BIRTH:
* The couple were unable to have children until an angel spoke to Zechariah.
* Both husband and wife were too old to have children.

A man who had been struck dumb was able to speak after his baby was named.

After the baby was eight days old, the mother told people that the baby was to be called John.

There is no one in the family with this name. They did not call him Zechariah after the father, which is the normal custom.

When they asked the father what he wanted to call the baby, he wrote the name 'John' on a stone tablet. At that moment, he was able to speak and was full of praise for God. The neighbours were surprised and afraid by what happened. Is there something special about this baby?

Family watch as father writes the baby's name on a stone tablet. Picture: Neil Stewart

MAN'S EAR CUT OFF IN FIT OF RAGE

A violent scene took place last night in the Garden of Gethsemane.

A crowd armed with swords and clubs were sent to arrest the man called Jesus. He had been holding a meeting with his followers at the time. A former follower, Judas Iscariot, had agreed to betray Jesus to earn money. For a long time the Chief Priests hated Jesus and were looking for an excuse to have him killed.

As the soldiers stepped forward to grab Jesus, one of his followers took a sword and cut off the ear of a man standing nearby. This man was the servant of the High Priest. Jesus did not want this violent behaviour to continue. He put out his hand and healed the servant's ear. Jesus' followers then ran off and left him alone with the crowd of soldiers. He was taken to the High Priest's house where the trial continues.

Pictures: Neil Pinchbeck

Friends and family gather outside Lazarus' tomb. Picture: Neil Pinchbeck

MAN RISES FROM THE DEAD

The small town of Bethany is buzzing with excitement after a man came back to life.

Two sisters, Martha and Mary, were distressed by their brother Lazarus' sudden illness. They tried to contact Jesus and asked him to come at once. However, he chose not to visit his sick friend immediately. Lazarus had been dead and been buried for four days before Jesus arrived.

When Jesus saw how upset the family were, he too started to cry. He asked to be taken to Lazarus' grave, which was a tomb with a large stone placed in front of it.

(story continued on page 34)

MAN RISES FROM THE DEAD
(continued from page 33)

Many people were upset that Jesus had not come more quickly, believing that he could have healed Lazarus.

However, Jesus told the people that the death had happened for a purpose - to bring glory to God. Then he ordered that the stone was to be removed. The crowd were horrified and worried that there would be a terrible smell.

After the stone was taken away, Jesus prayed to God. Then speaking in a loud voice he shouted for Lazarus to come out of the tomb.

As the crowd watched in amazement, Lazarus came alive. Many people have turned to God and now believe in Jesus' teaching.

BURIAL TRADITIONS

*   After death, bodies are normally prepared for burial by being washed, covered in oils and spices and wrapped in cloth like linen.

*   It is traditional for people to be buried in the same tomb as others of the family if this is possible.

*   The most usual burial-places are caves, or tombs cut out of the rock.

*   The raising of Lazarus is not usual and was caused by a miracle.

Picture: Neil Pinchbeck

Picture: Neil Pinchbeck

Hi readers!

Thanks for all your letters this week. I'm sorry that we only have enough room to print two letters in this issue, I'll make sure you get a reply as soon as possible.

Dear Uncle Josh,

I spend a lot of time worrying about things. Just recently I heard that the man called Jesus is telling people not to worry. I find this hard to understand. How can I stop being afraid?
Best wishes,

I. Worry-a-Lot.

Dear Uncle Josh,

I heard my Father say that Jesus is the Son of God. I thought Joseph the carpenter was his Dad. Does he have two Fathers?

Puzzled wishes,
Samuel

Dear I. Worry-a-Lot,

Jesus has a good reason not to worry. He tells us that God in heaven will take care of those who trust in him. God looks after the birds of the air and flowers in the fields. You are much more special to him! He will make sure you have enough food to eat and clothes to wear.

The way to stop worrying is to ask God to help you, and he will!
Hope this helps.
Uncle Josh.

PS: Remember though, God will give you what you *need* - not everything you would like to have!

Dear Sam,

I can quite understand why you are confused. People called Christians believe that Jesus is the Son of God and that he came into the world so that we can be friends with God.

This makes Joseph the carpenter Jesus' legal guardian.

Uncle Josh

STRANGE DARKNESS COVERS LAND

Picture: Fred Apps

An unusual event took place yesterday when the whole land was covered in darkness.

The darkness lasted for three hours until 3 o'clock. At the same time a curtain in the temple was ripped in two pieces. Both events happened around the time that Jesus of Nazareth was killed on the cross.

The famous prophet was sentenced to death after the crowd persuaded Pilate to have him killed. Pilate tried to tell the people that Jesus had not committed a crime, but the crowd would not listen.

Jesus had been accused of talking against God and making claims which were not true. He was beaten and handed over to Pilate who ordered him to be crucified.

Jesus has become known throughout the country for performing amazing miracles. Many people wondered if Jesus would be able to come down off

Jesus has become known throughout the country for performing amazing miracles.

'This man was really the Son of God!'

the cross and save himself.

However, it has been predicted that Jesus was to die for a special purpose. He claimed that his death would take away people's sin and give them the chance to be friends with God.

Followers of Jesus are said to be suffering shock from this loss. Even those who did not believe what Jesus taught have been affected. One army officer who watched the event is reported to have said, 'This man was really the Son of God!'

A man called Joseph from Arimathea, asked permission to have Jesus' body buried in a tomb of solid rock. A huge stone was placed in front of the tomb and soldiers were told to guard the area.

Jesus has been reported to have healed many people

Some of the problems which he cured were:
* Leprosy
* Lameness
* Blindness
* Dumbness
* Fevers
* Demon-possession
* Deformed limbs

Some of the people he cured were:
* Simon Peter's mother-in-law
* Blind Bartimaeus
* Malchus (the High Priest's servant)
* Lazarus
* Jairus' daughter
* A Roman officer's servant

WHO IS HE?

He heals people who are sick.
He brings people back from the dead.
He makes amazing claims.

In case you haven't already guessed, this week's feature article is about the man called Jesus.

PERSONAL PROFILE:

Place of birth: Bethlehem

Mother's name: Mary

Place of upbringing: Nazareth

Notes: Taken to Egypt soon after he was born.
Baptised in the River Jordan by John Baptist.
Performed many amazing miracles.
Made startling claims.

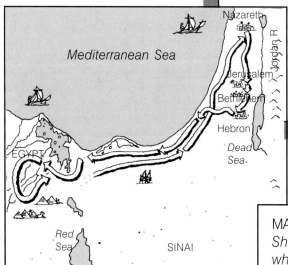

MAP
Showing the route which Mary and Joseph would have taken to go from Bethlehem to Egypt and back to Nazareth.